monday morning®

Paper Plates

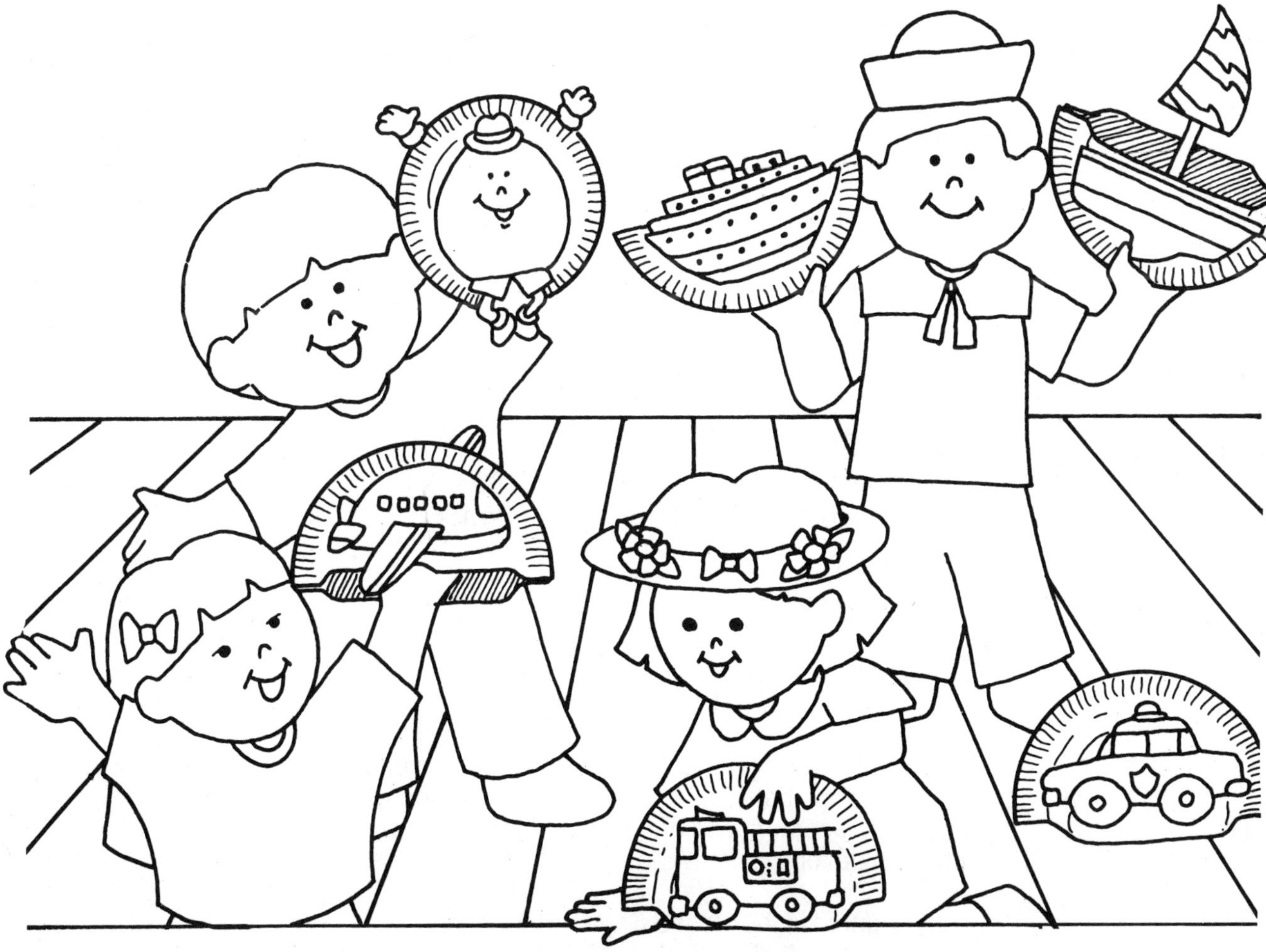

by Marilynn G. Barr

Publisher: Roberta Suid
Editor: Carol Whiteley
Production: Susan Cronin-Paris

Related scissors skills books from Monday Morning
Books: *Hangups, Gift Fun, Paper Crafts, ABC
Puppets, ABC Puzzles, ABC Art.*

ISBN 0-912107-99-5

Entire contents copyright © 1989
by Monday Morning Books, Inc., Box 1680,
Palo Alto, California 94302

monday
morning®
Monday Morning is a registered trademark of
Monday Morning Books, Inc.

Printed in the United States of America
9 8 7 6 5 4 3 2 1

CONTENTS

INTRODUCTION

Paper Plates was designed to provide young children ages three to six with the opportunity to use scissors skills to develop eye-hand coordination, fine-motor skills, and visual perception; the activities also give children experience in directional follow-through and organization. To create the crafts, children cut out patterns, then color, decorate, and paste them to paper plates or paper cups. The activity themes range from nursery rhymes to animals to holidays and transportation. All projects foster the language arts as well as integrate with other curriculum areas.

Getting Ready

To work successfully with these activities, children should be fairly comfortable using scissors. They should be able to hold the scissors correctly and open and close it to cut. For those who need to develop better cutting skills, provide practice with training scissors. Have the children cut large shapes from construction paper, wallpaper, magazine covers, or brown paper bags. Allow left-handers to use left-handed scissors.

To refine cutting skills, have the children cut along thick felt-pen lines—straight or gently curving. Make the cutting lines narrower as the children progress. Also glue a series of stars on construction paper, or make a series of large felt-pen dots closely spaced at first, then farther apart. Have the children cut from star to star or dot to dot. Then have the children cut out large squares, rectangles, and triangles, showing them how to turn the paper or their hands as they cut. Finally, have the children cut out more complicated shapes, such as circles, semi-circles, and irregular shapes. Let the children make collages from the shapes they cut out, or have them paste the shapes onto boxes to make colorful storage or gift containers.

Making the Crafts

Begin by reproducing the patterns for each activity. Then have the children cut out the simple shapes by following the dotted cutting lines. Finally, have the children color, decorate, and paste the patterns onto paper plates or paper cups. Direction symbols appear at the top of the pattern sheets to guide the children and help them toward independent follow-through. Materials needed to make each set of projects are listed below, and a small diagram of the completed activity is given on some pages. Enrichment ideas for using the projects are suggested below.

Nursery Rhyme Puppets—

Materials: patterns, scissors, paste or glue stick, crayons, stapler, large white paper or Styrofoam plates, large white paper or Styrofoam plates cut in half

Have the children cut out the nursery rhyme patterns and color them in. Then have them paste each pattern to a whole paper plate. Staple a half plate to the back upper half of the whole plate to form a pocket for the child's hand. Show the children where to paste special features such as wings, hands, or paws, and have them try out their puppets by slipping their hand into the pocket, holding it between their fingers and thumb.

Farm Animal Puppets—

Materials: patterns, scissors, paste or glue stick, crayons, medium-size paper cups

Have the children cut out the farmer and the farm animal patterns and color them in. Then have them paste each pattern to a paper cup, pasting the patterns down the center so the sides are not attached to the cup. Children can use the paper cup puppets by slipping their hand into the cup or by holding the sides of the cup and moving the puppets around.

Holiday Gifts and Ornaments—

Materials: patterns, scissors, paste or glue stick, crayons, medium-size paper cups, large and small white paper or Styrofoam plates, drinking straws, yarn or ribbon, stapler, yellow tissue paper, hole punch, tape, glitter (optional)

Have the children cut out the patterns for the gifts and ornaments, then color and decorate them. Then have them paste each pattern onto a paper plate or paper cup under your direction. Follow the picture diagrams and directions on the pattern pages. Staple yarn or ribbon to wreaths and hats.

Paper Plate Vehicles—

Materials: patterns, scissors, paste or glue stick, crayons, large white paper or Styrofoam plates cut in half, stapler, bottle caps or Tinkertoy wheels

Have the children cut out both sides of each vehicle and color them in. Then staple together two paper plate halves. With the open side as the bottom of the vehicle, have the children paste the vehicle, back and front, to the plate halves. Bottle cap or Tinkertoy wheels can then be glued onto wheeled vehicles. To use the vehicles, the children should stand them up and move them along the floor or a table top.

Enrichment

Nursery Rhyme Puppets—

Let the children move the puppets to nursery rhymes or songs with appropriate actions. They can also put on a puppet play for another class as part of a Nursery Rhyme Party. The puppets can also be used to generate imaginative, spontaneous stories or original lines to add to nursery rhyme favorites. Number and time concepts, vocabulary, rhyming, and figurative expressions can also be discussed.

Here are additional enrichment ideas for specific puppets:

Bring out Humpty Dumpty at Easter time to display among decorated eggs; present a unit covering the development of the egg to the chick, including the incubation of eggs and the graphing of chick growth. Talk about Old King Cole as well as real kings, and have a king and queen of the week for a self-esteem booster. Ask each king and queen to bring in a baby picture to share. For the Crooked Man, use masking tape to make a crooked path on the floor for everyone to walk on. Have Mary and her little lambs come to school one day and make the children laugh and play. For Little Jack Horner, give each child a pie plate with a purple paper plum; the children can stick in their thumb and

pull out a plum! Have the children act out Little Boy Blue with a pile of hay or a painted paper haystack for a backdrop. Some children can pretend to fall asleep "at the hay" and then Mary's little lambs can come baaa-ing and try to wake them up! Have the children think up more things to do and create with the nursery rhymes and puppets.

Farm Animal Puppets–

Have the children move the puppets to the song "Old McDonald Had a Farm," making the appropriate sounds for each animal. The puppets will help the children remember the sequence of the song. Everyone should have a turn taking the part of the farmer. You can also outline or paint a farm scene on a large piece of paper and have the children use dramatic play to show work and life on the farm, creating dialogue between the farmer and the animals. A special treat would be a trip to a real farm for first-hand animal experience, or the children might like to make a Farm Animal Book in which they paste copies of the animal patterns. The children could dictate simple stories for each animal to be included in the book.

Holiday Gifts and Ornaments—

Accompany the holiday crafts with games, songs, dances, poems, and stories. Use pumpkin face masks to act out "Five Little Pumpkins," or have the children make "ghosty" sounds or act out ghost stories with the Push-up Ghost Puppet. Use the Christmas centerpiece, wreath, and Hanukkah candles to decorate the classroom or use as props while learning songs and poems or listening to stories for each festive event. The children may also wrap up their creations in colorful tissue paper and ribbons and take them home as gifts for the family.

Valentine cards can be slipped into valentine paper plate mailboxes that are taped to the children's desks. The boxes also make great containers for fresh flowers or handmade valentine gifts.

At Easter, let the girls wear their paper plate Easter bonnets and parade to the tune of "The Easter Parade," with the boys as their escorts. Or the children could have a pretend spring garden party with songs, dances, games, and real punch and cookies. In their St. Patrick's Day hats, they could bid each other "Top o' the mornin'!" and dance a jig. If you paint a colorful rainbow on a large piece of paper, tape it to the wall, and place a pot of gold (circles of yellow construction paper) at one end, the children can pretend they're leprechauns and dance around. Tell a tricky story about a clever leprechaun for the children to act out.

Mom, Dad, and the grandparents will delight in their "special day" gifts. Mom might want to use her flower wreath as a centerpiece for flowers, candy, or nuts. Dad might pretend to eat his hero sandwich, then save it for later restaurant play. The grandparents will enjoy the sunflower plate they receive, especially if it has the giver's photo taped to it.

Finally, what would a party be without a paper plate cone-shaped party hat! Have the children decorate their hats with stickers, ribbons, or glitter, and celebrate a special birthday with punch and cupcakes and a birthday candle. The hats can also be used when the class brings in the New Year with a parade and noisemakers. A cone hat with the tip cut off makes a wonderful megaphone or bugle for announcements or celebrating.

Paper Plate Vehicles—

Children will enjoy using the paper plate vehicles in active play. You can paint a floor map of towns, roads, harbors, bays, and airports on a large piece of paper and let the children move the vehicles around, racing the fire truck to put out a fire or loading the school bus with children and going to the zoo. You could also talk about—and perhaps solve!—traffic problems as the children manipulate their vehicles. Water transport could focus on a cruise around the bay in the sailboat, or using the tugboat to guide the cruise ship into the harbor. Air travel study might include a discussion of how a hot air balloon works, and how the weather affects the way it flies.

To enhance the children's dramatic play, plan a visit to a close-by city, airport, fire station, or harbor. Arrange to have a real fire truck come to the school as part of a unit on fire safety. You could also show films about various vehicles, or have the children dictate stories about the paper plate vehicles. In discussion, the children could find similarities and differences among the vehicles, and tell what each can do. Make up some riddles and ask the children to guess which vehicle a riddle is about. You can also use the cars as props in plays or for a display on transportation for other classes to see.

As the children work with the activities in this book, they will generate many more ideas and ways to use the crafts. Let them have free rein in their imaginative and spontaneous play. The positive motivation and activity will foster learning and all-around growth.

by Lillian Lieberman

Humpty Dumpty
Humpty Dumpty sat on a wall,
Humpty Dumpty had a great fall.

Old King Cole

Old King Cole was a merry old soul,
And a merry old soul was he;

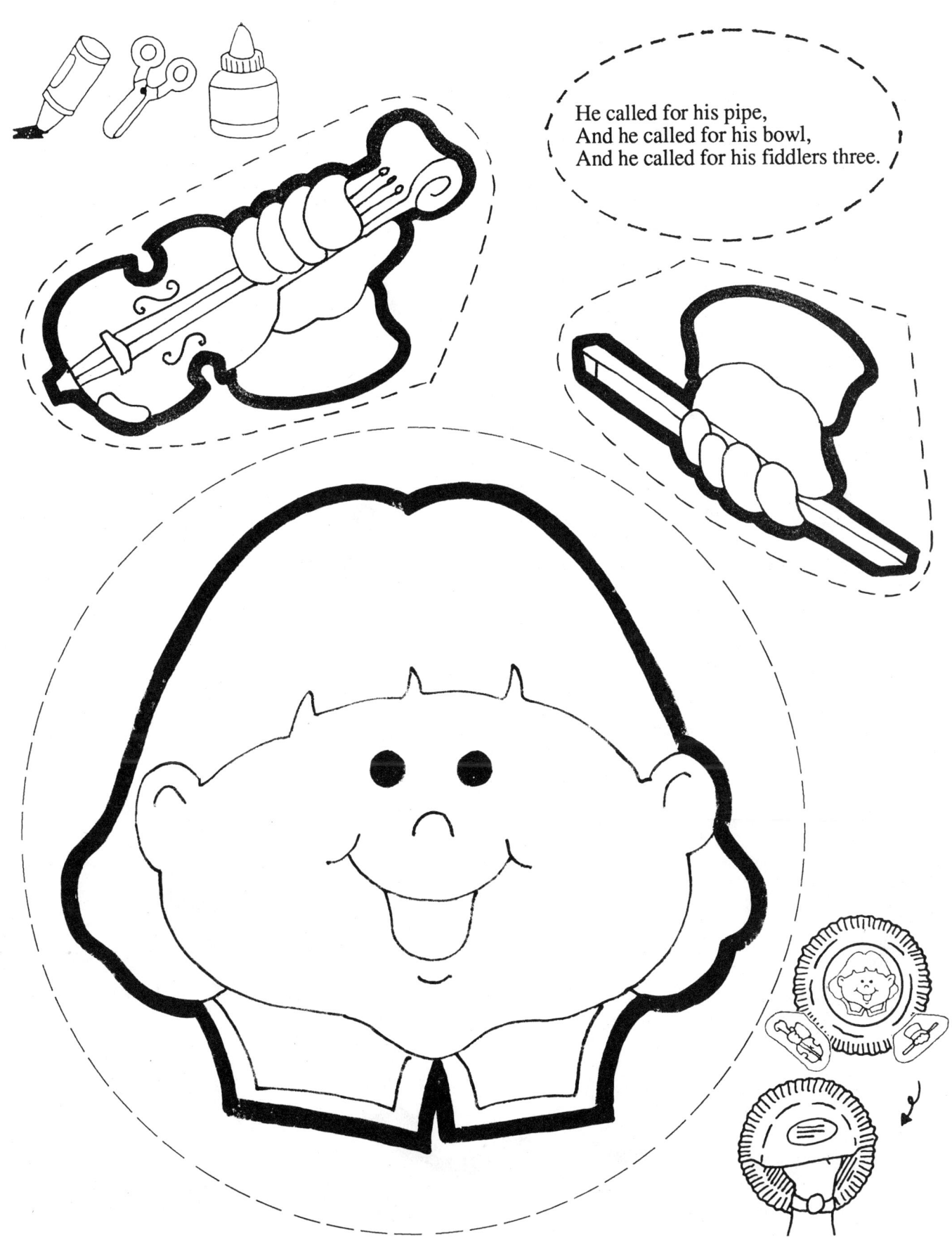

He called for his pipe,
And he called for his bowl,
And he called for his fiddlers three.

**Mary Had
a Little Lamb**

Mary had a little lamb,
It's fleece was white as snow,
And everywhere that Mary went,
The lamb was sure to go.

It followed her to school one day, And made the children laugh and play.

Wee Willie Winkie

Wee Willie Winkie runs through the town,
Upstairs and downstairs, in his nightgown.

Little Boy Blue
Little boy blue come blow
your horn.
The sheep's in the meadow,
The cow's in the corn.

Where's the little boy that looks after the sheep? He's under the haystack fast asleep.

16

There Was a Crooked Man

There was a crooked man, and he
went a crooked mile;
He found a crooked sixpence
against a crooked stile;

He bought a crooked cat, which caught a crooked mouse;

18

And they all lived together in a little crooked house.

There Were Two Blackbirds

There were two blackbirds
sitting on a hill,
The one named Jack,
the other named Jill;

Fly away, Jack!
Fly away, Jill!
Come back, Jack!
Come back, Jill!

Little Jack Horner
Little Jack Horner sat in a corner
Eating his Christmas pie.
He put in his thumb and pulled
out a plum,
And said, "What a good
boy am I!"

22

Old
McDonald
Had A Farm

Quack

24

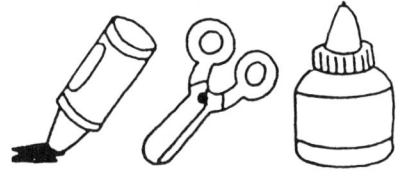

Moo

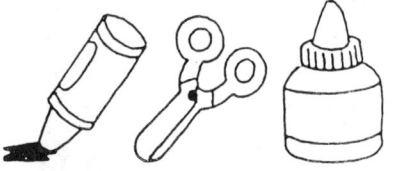

Neh

26

Oink

Meow

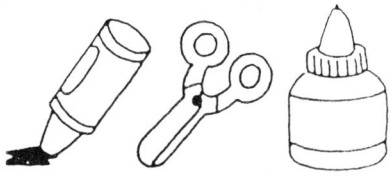

Bow-wow

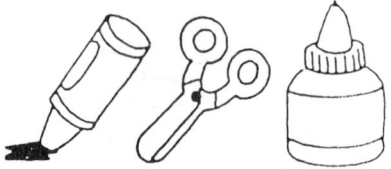

Baa

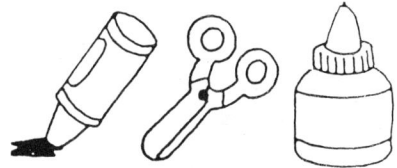

Naa

Cluck

Caw

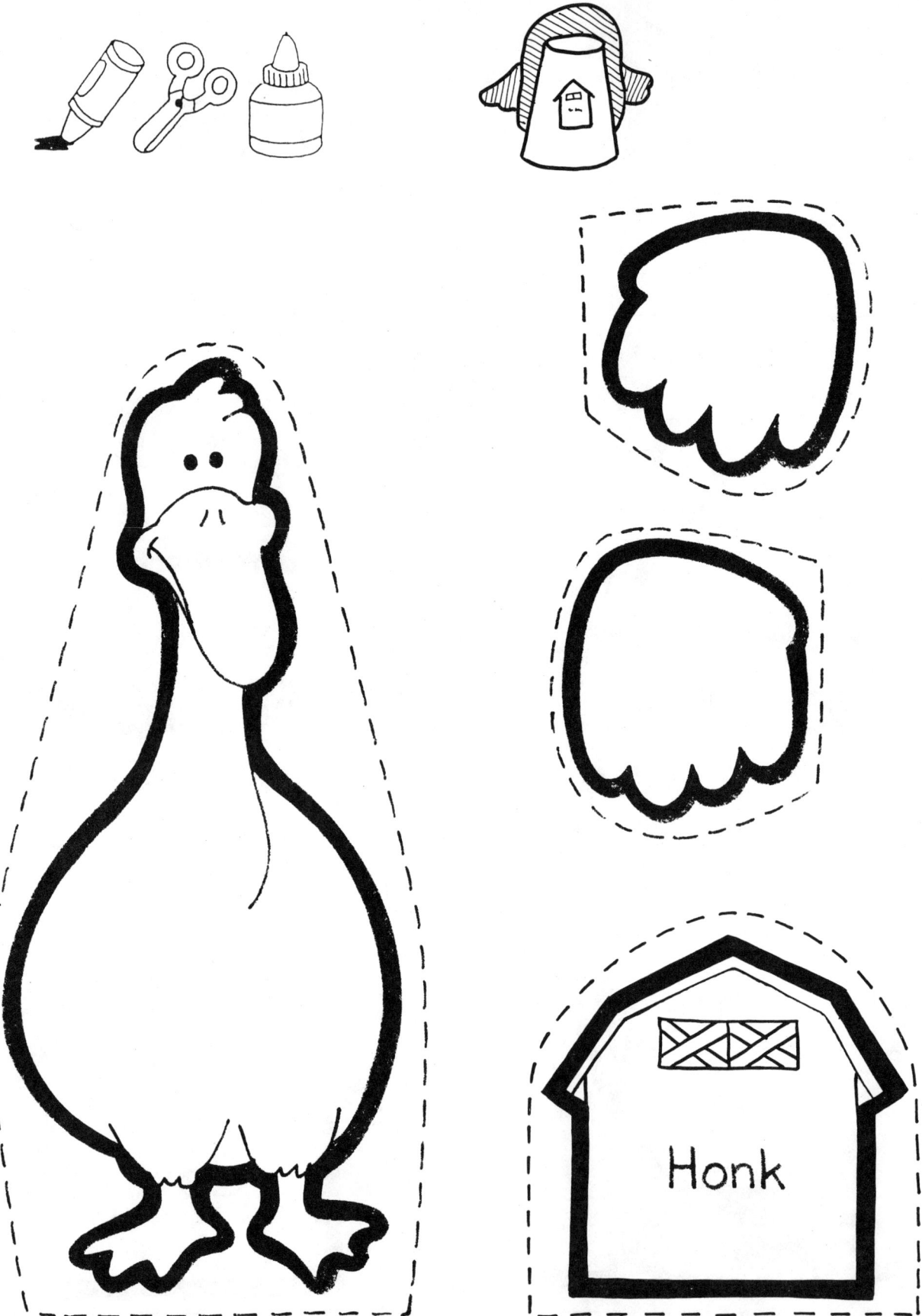

Honk

34

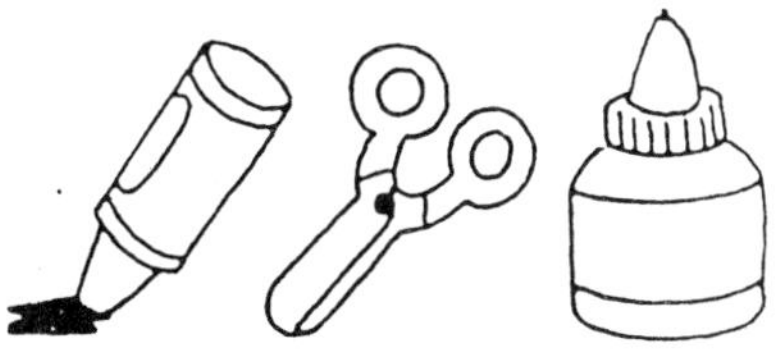

Hee-haw

Gobble

36

38

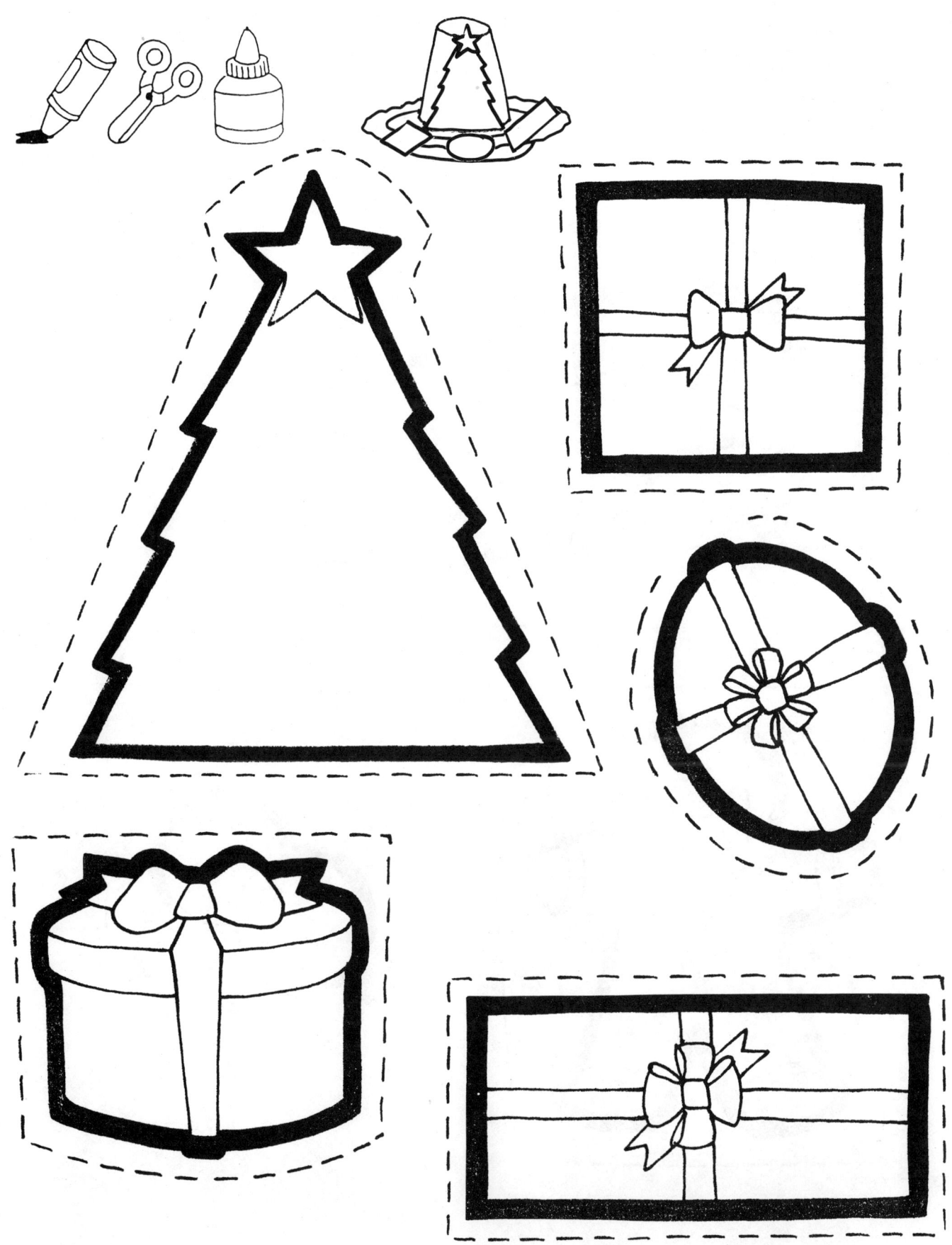

Note to Teacher:
Provide each child with three sets of patterns.

40

Note to Teacher:
Punch hole in each candle.
Provide each child with nine 1" squares of colored tissue paper to push through the flames.
Tape the tissue paper in the back to secure.

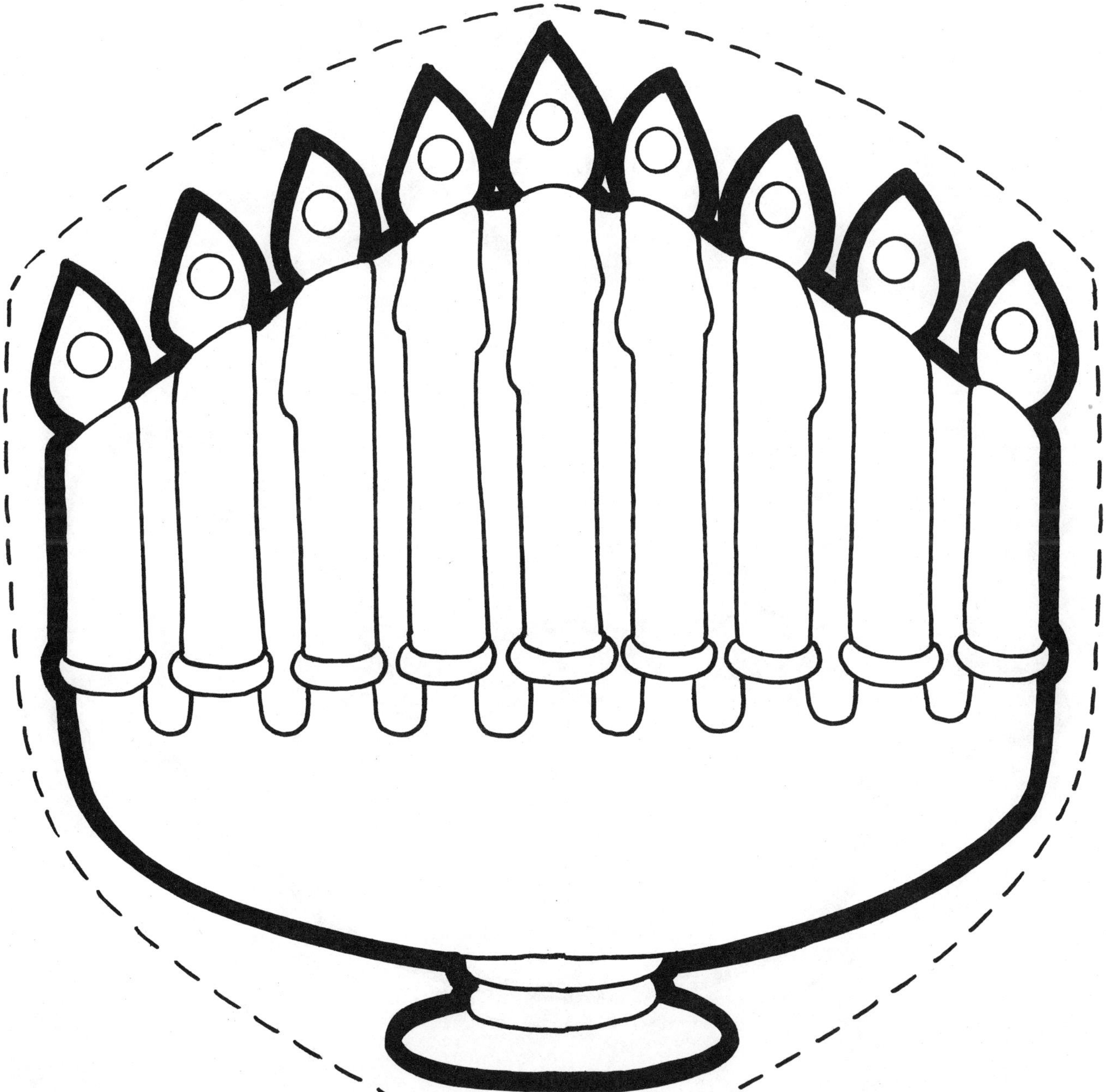

MY VALENTINES

43

44

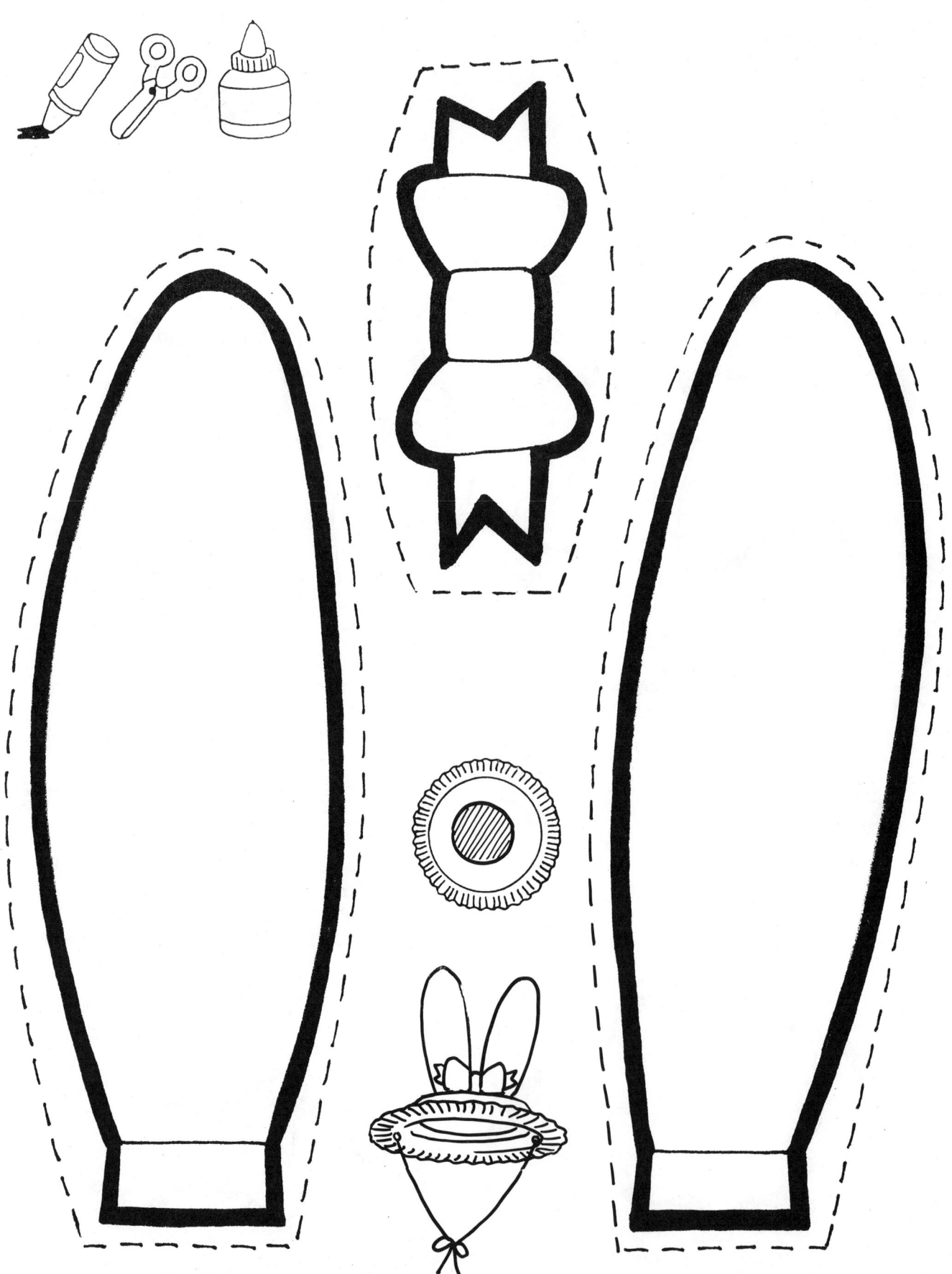

For My Hero

To:

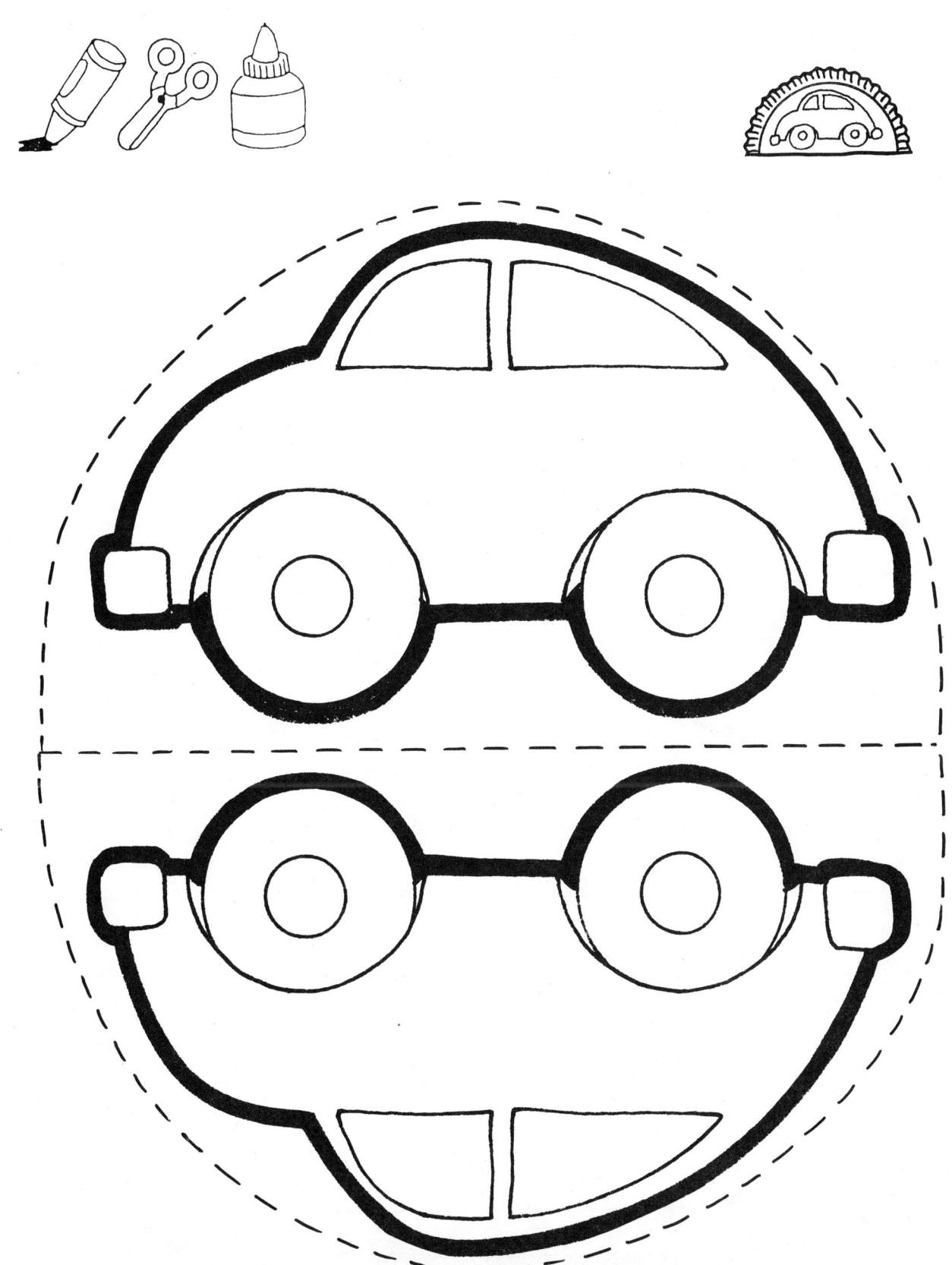

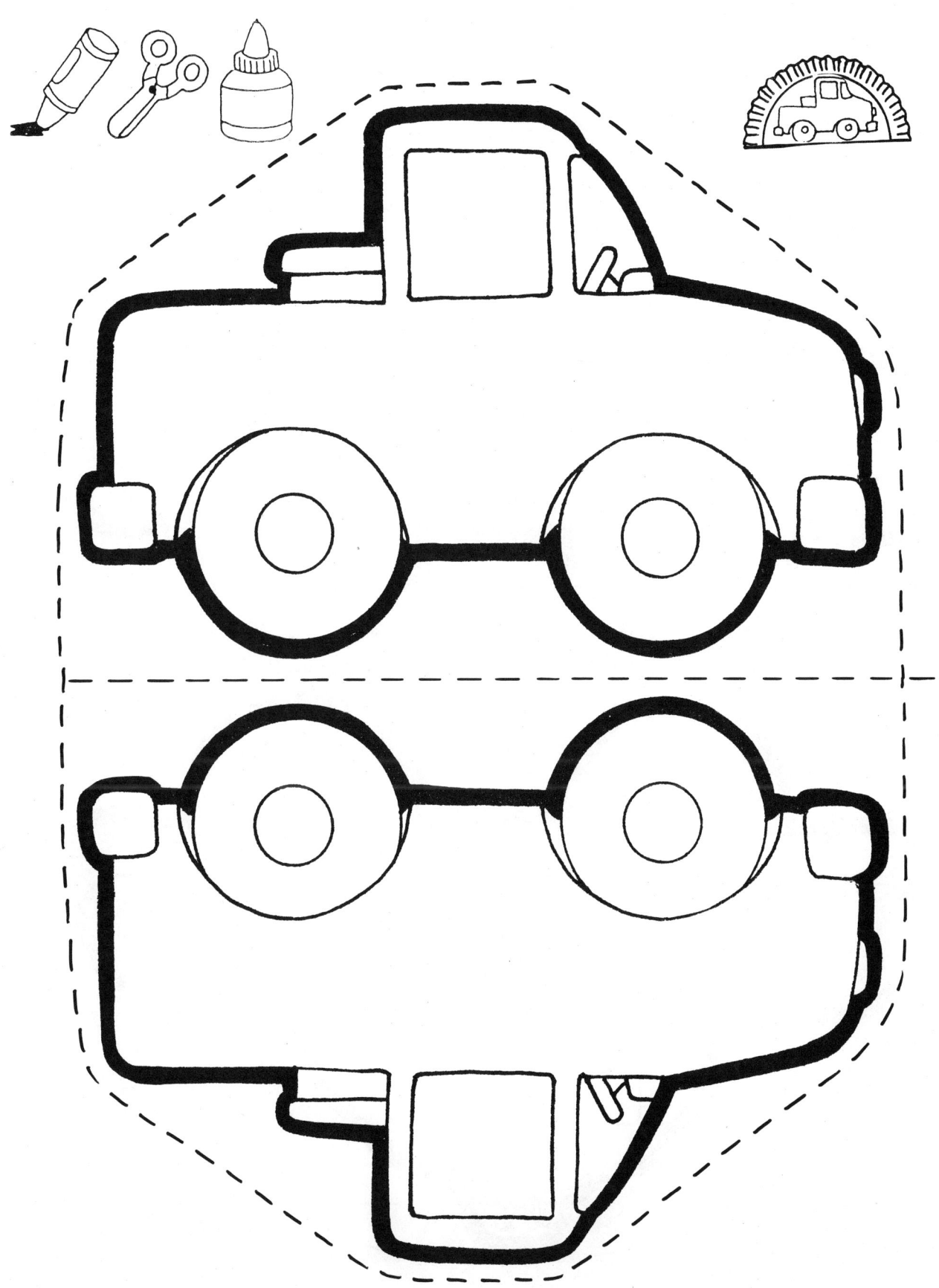

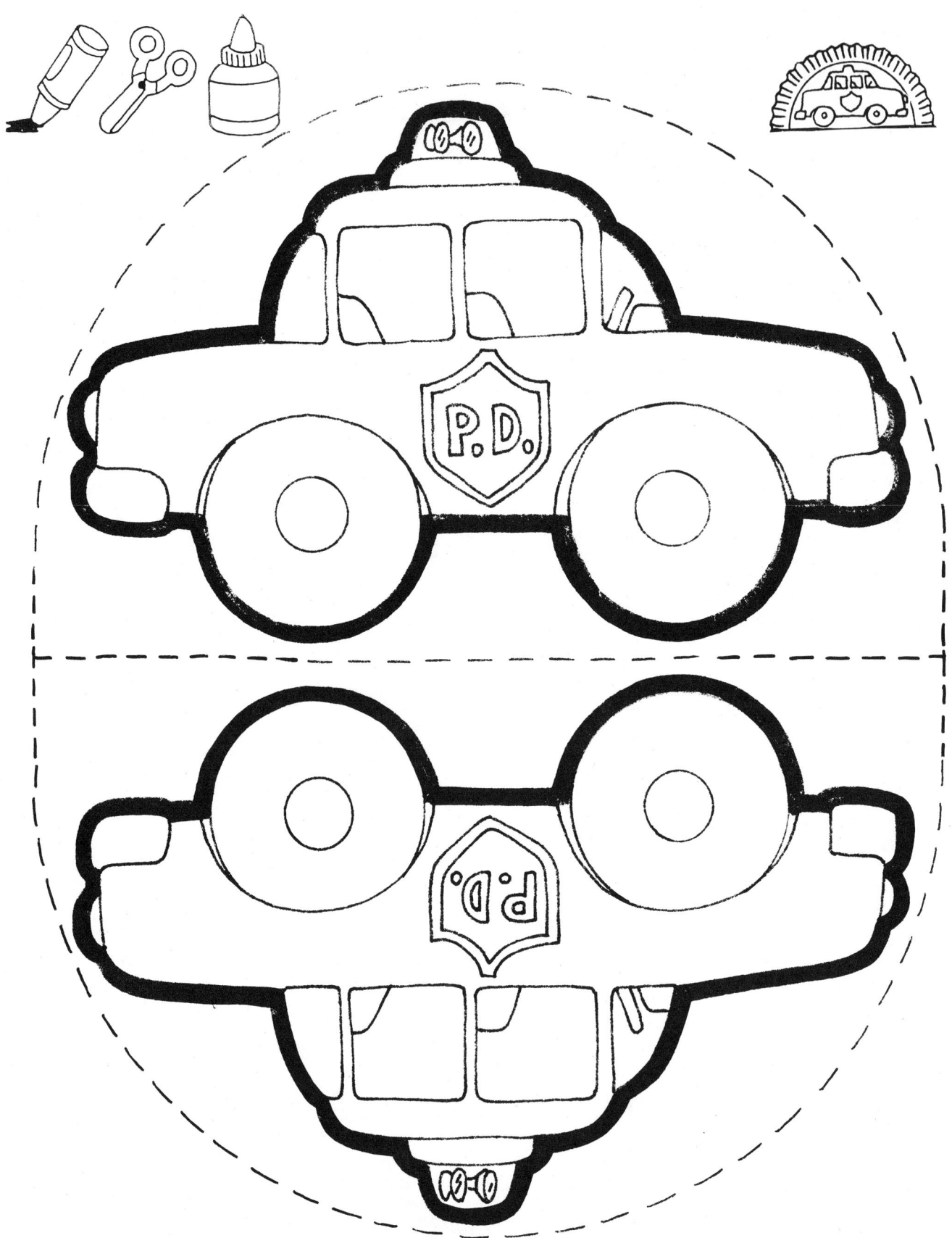

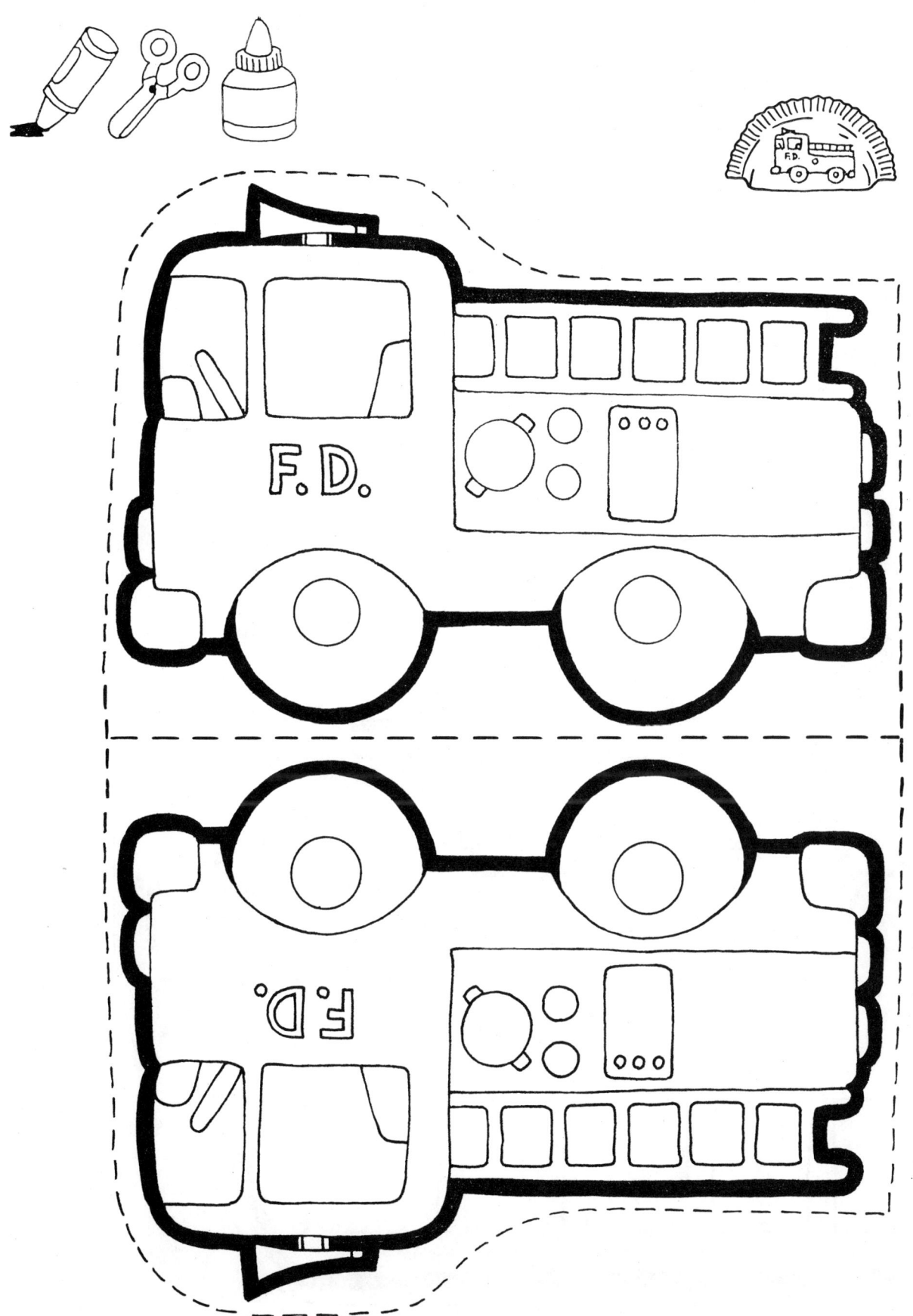

School Bus

STOP

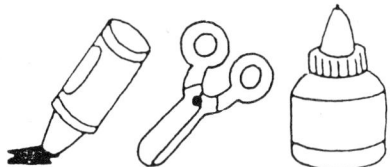 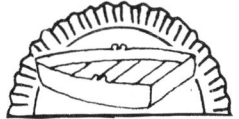

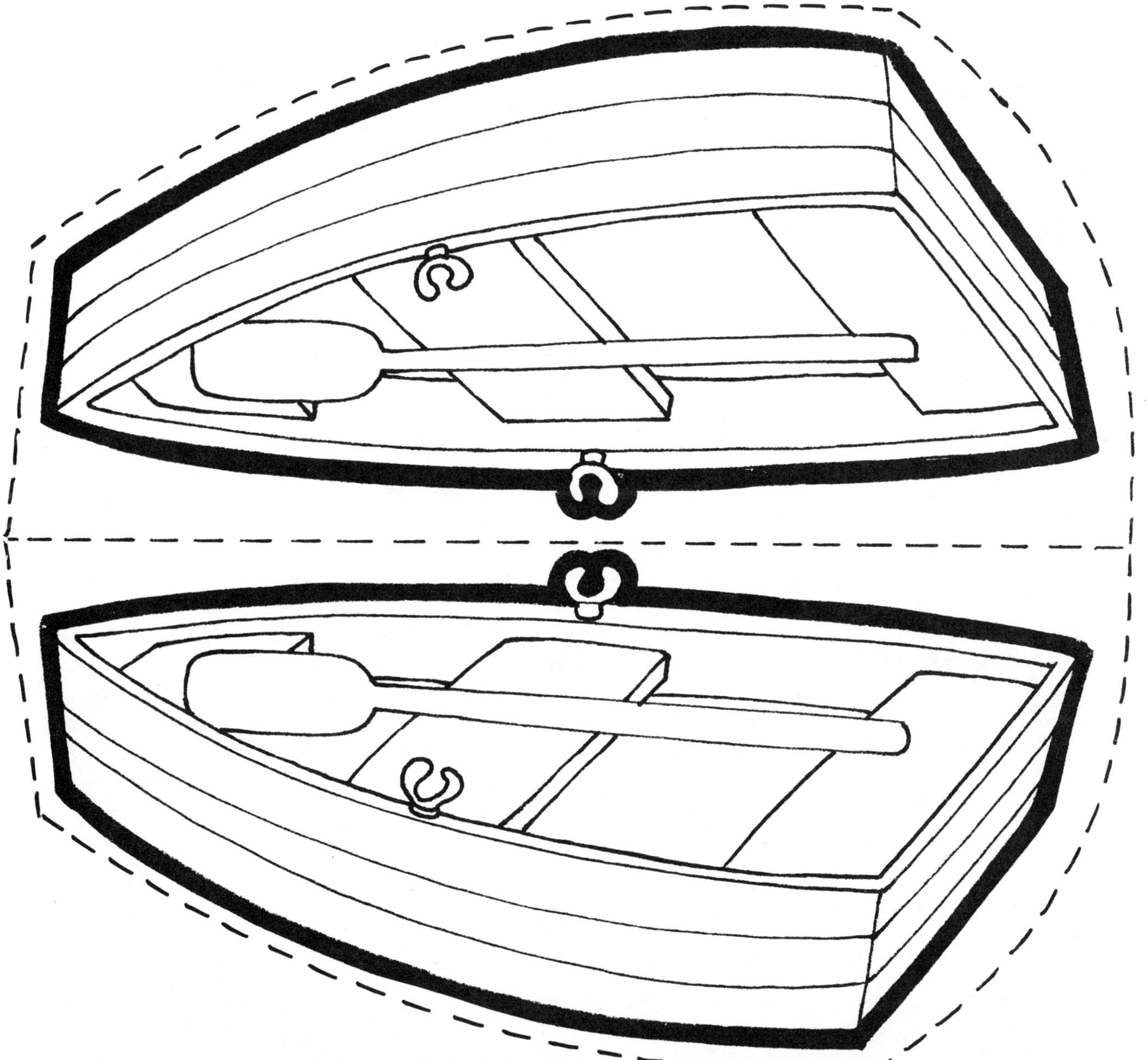

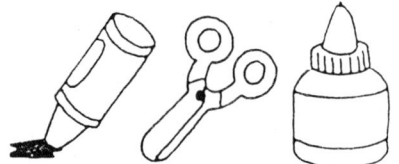

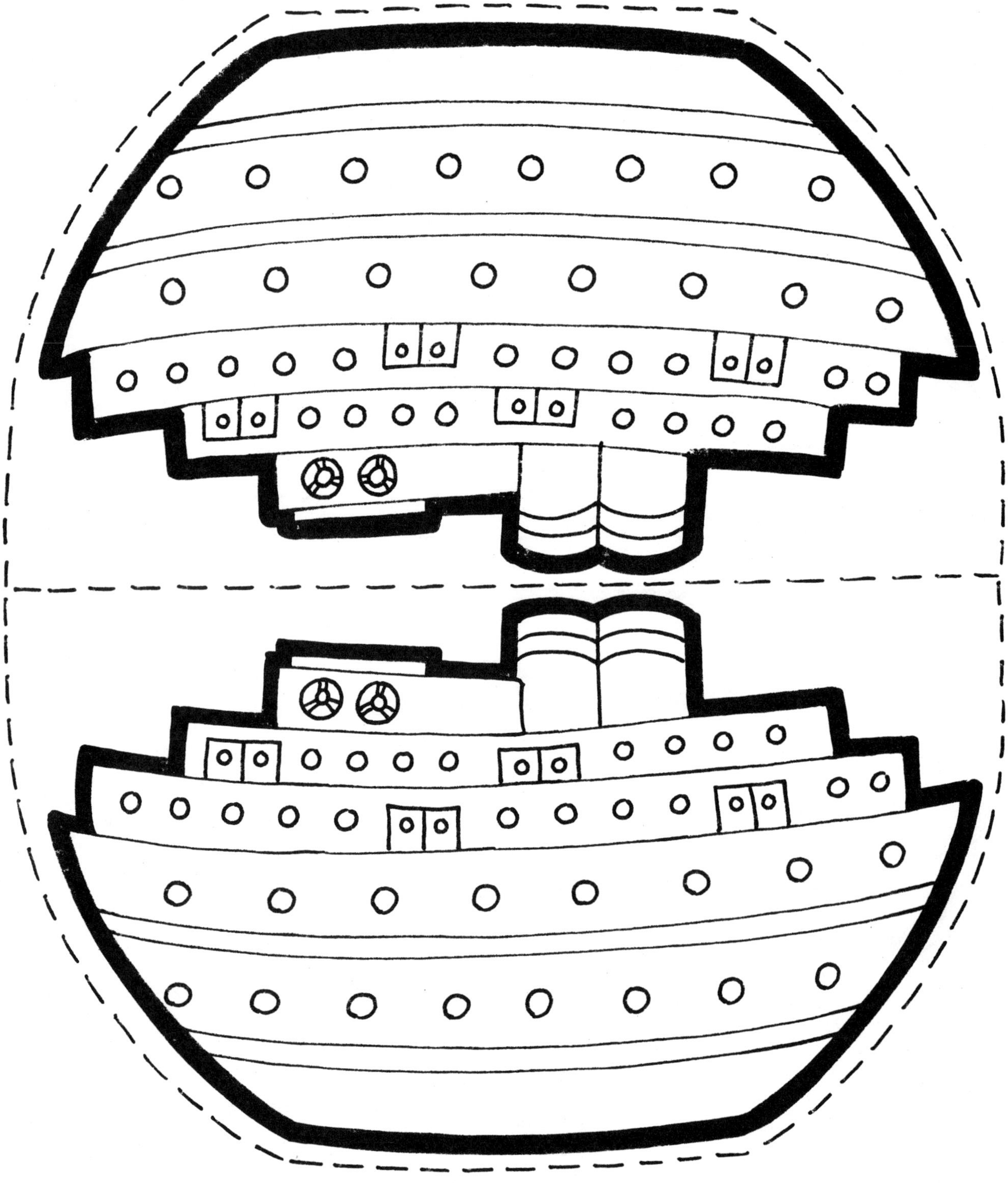

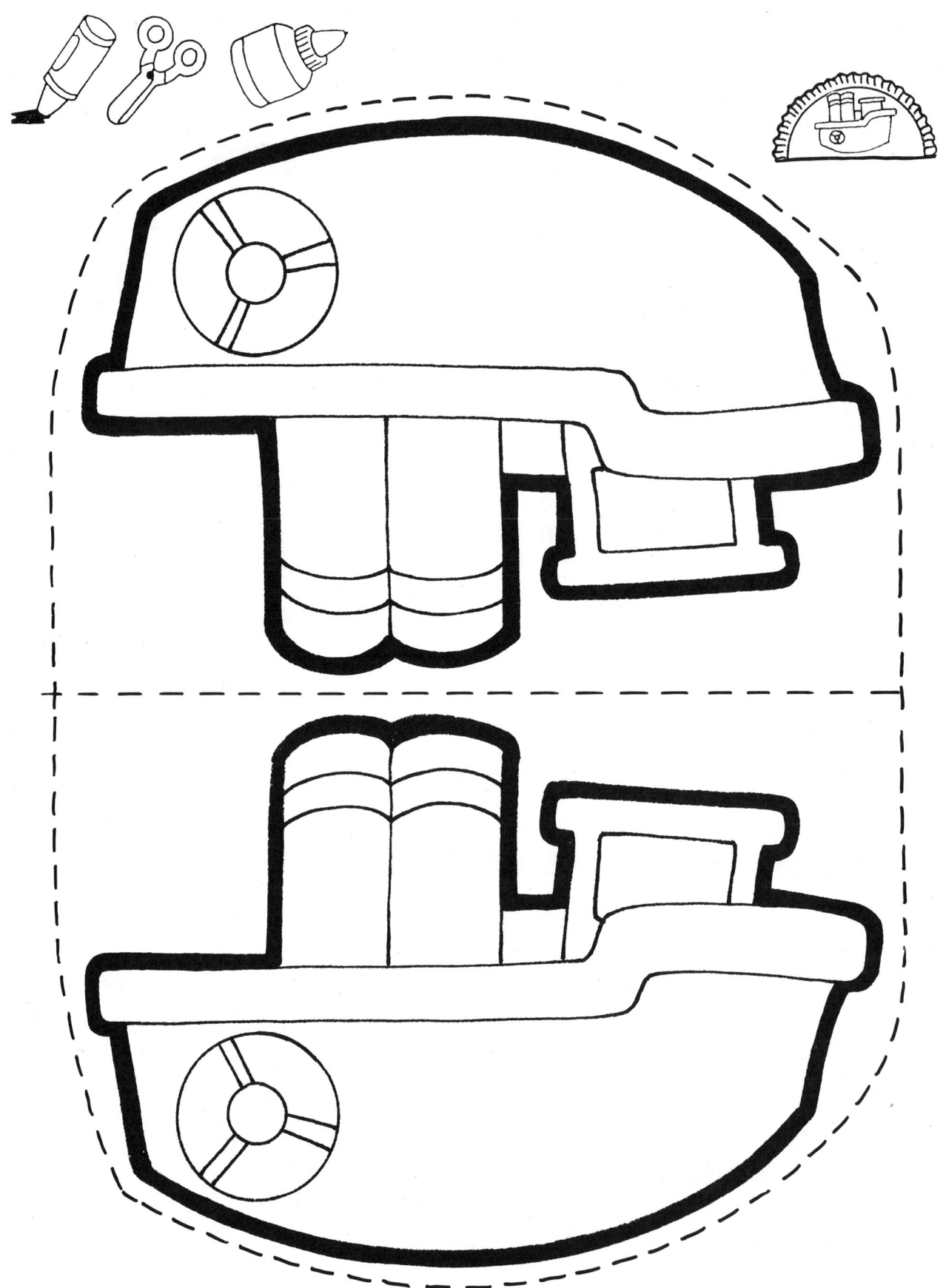

60

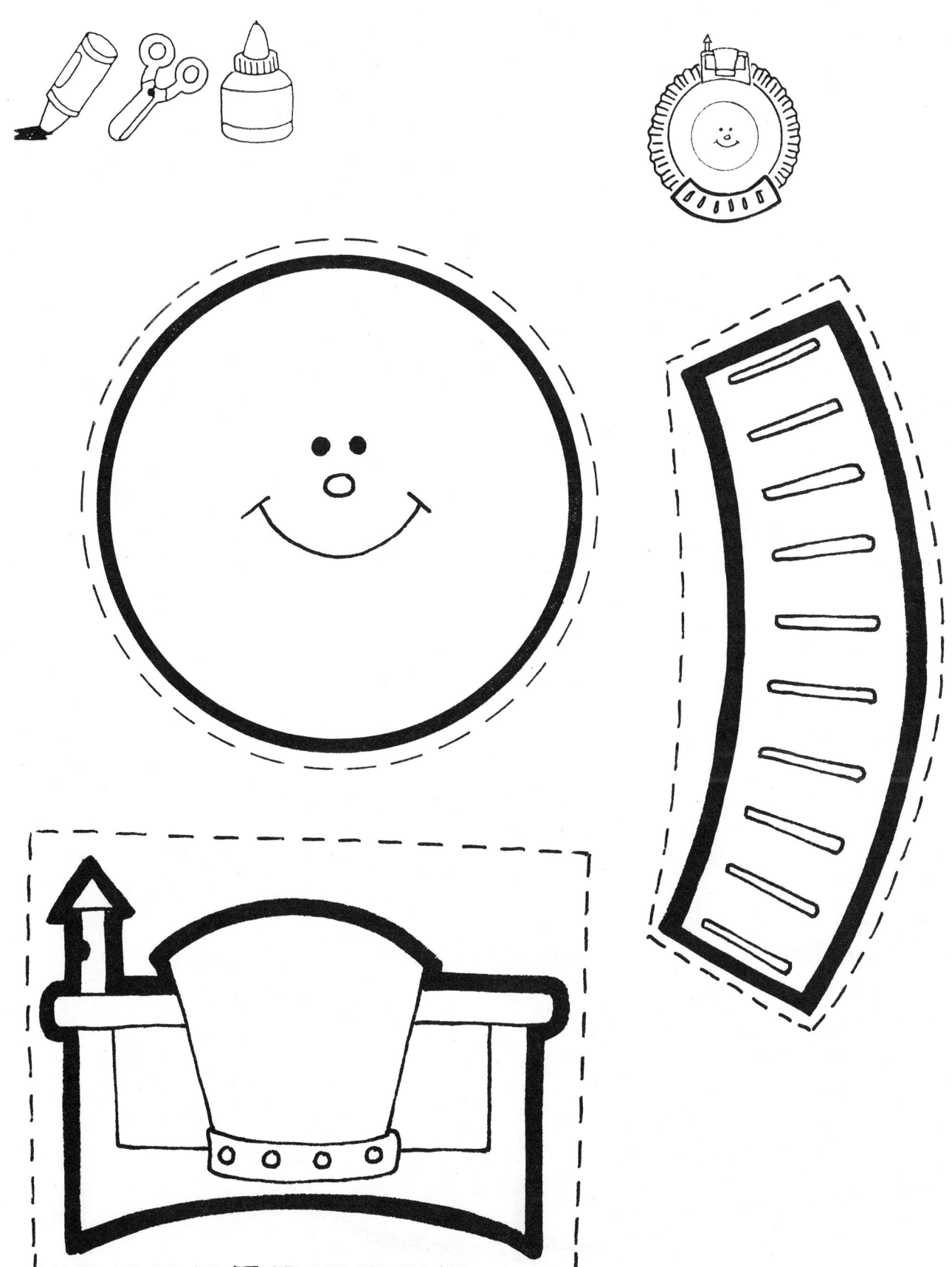

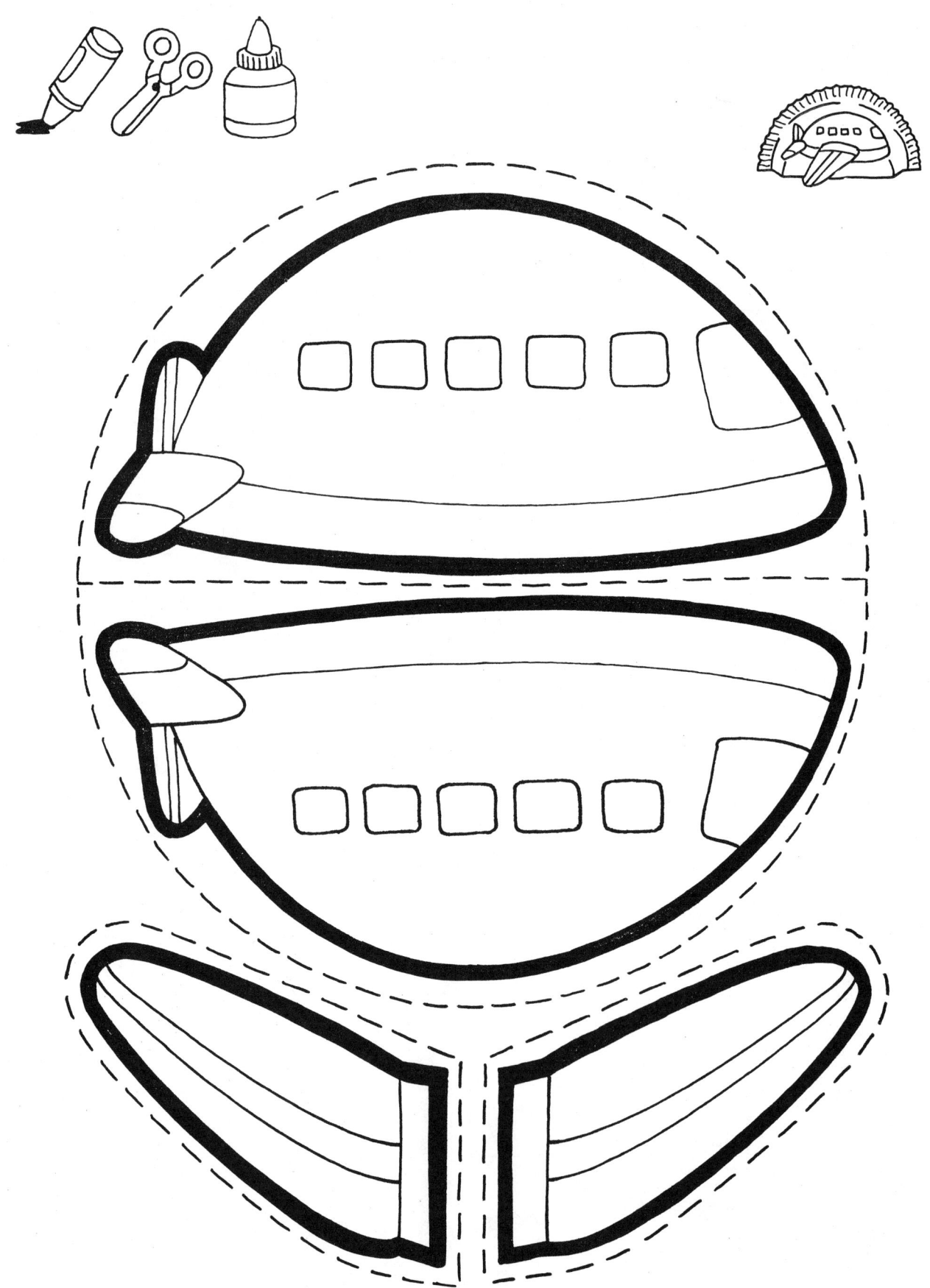

62

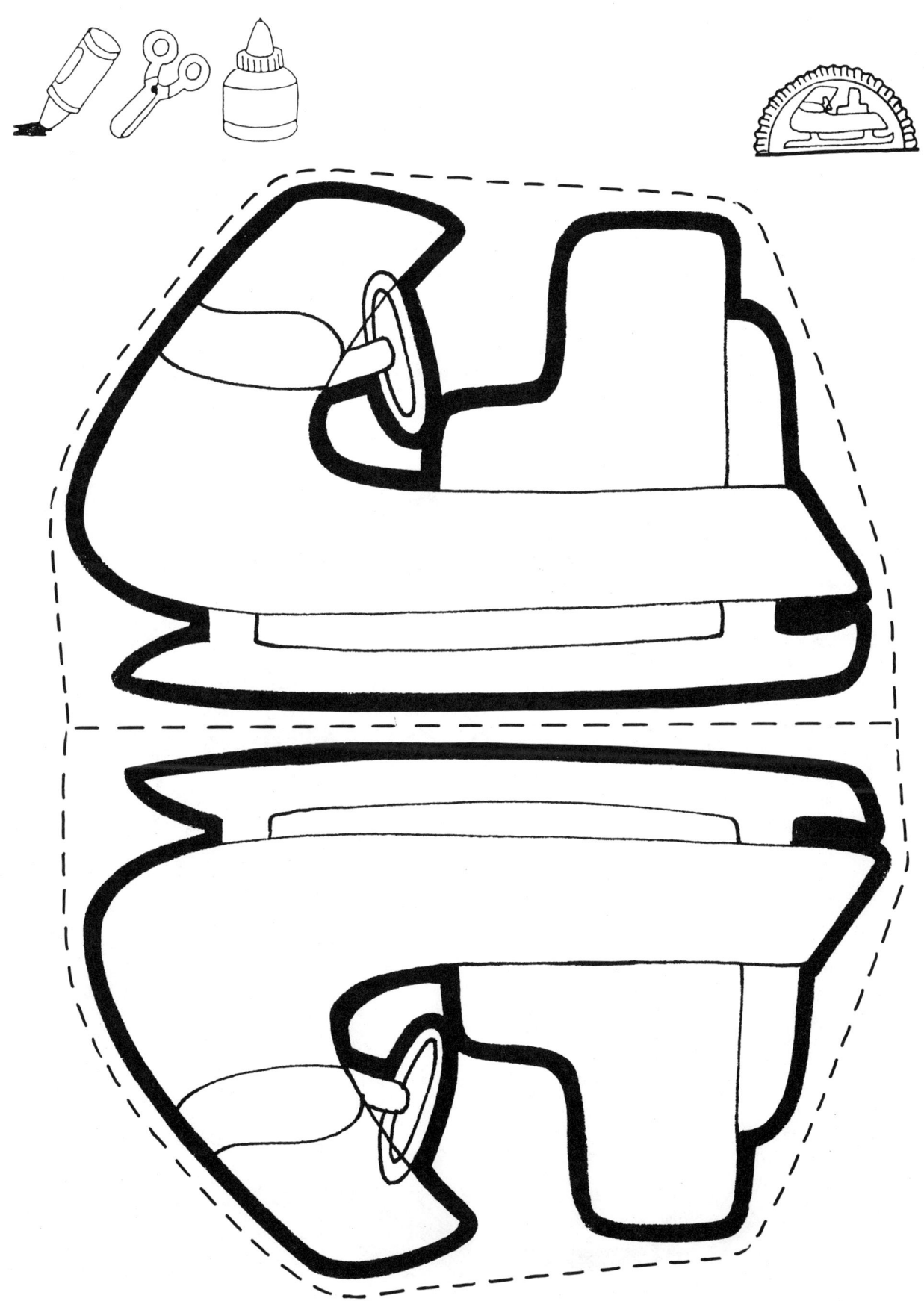

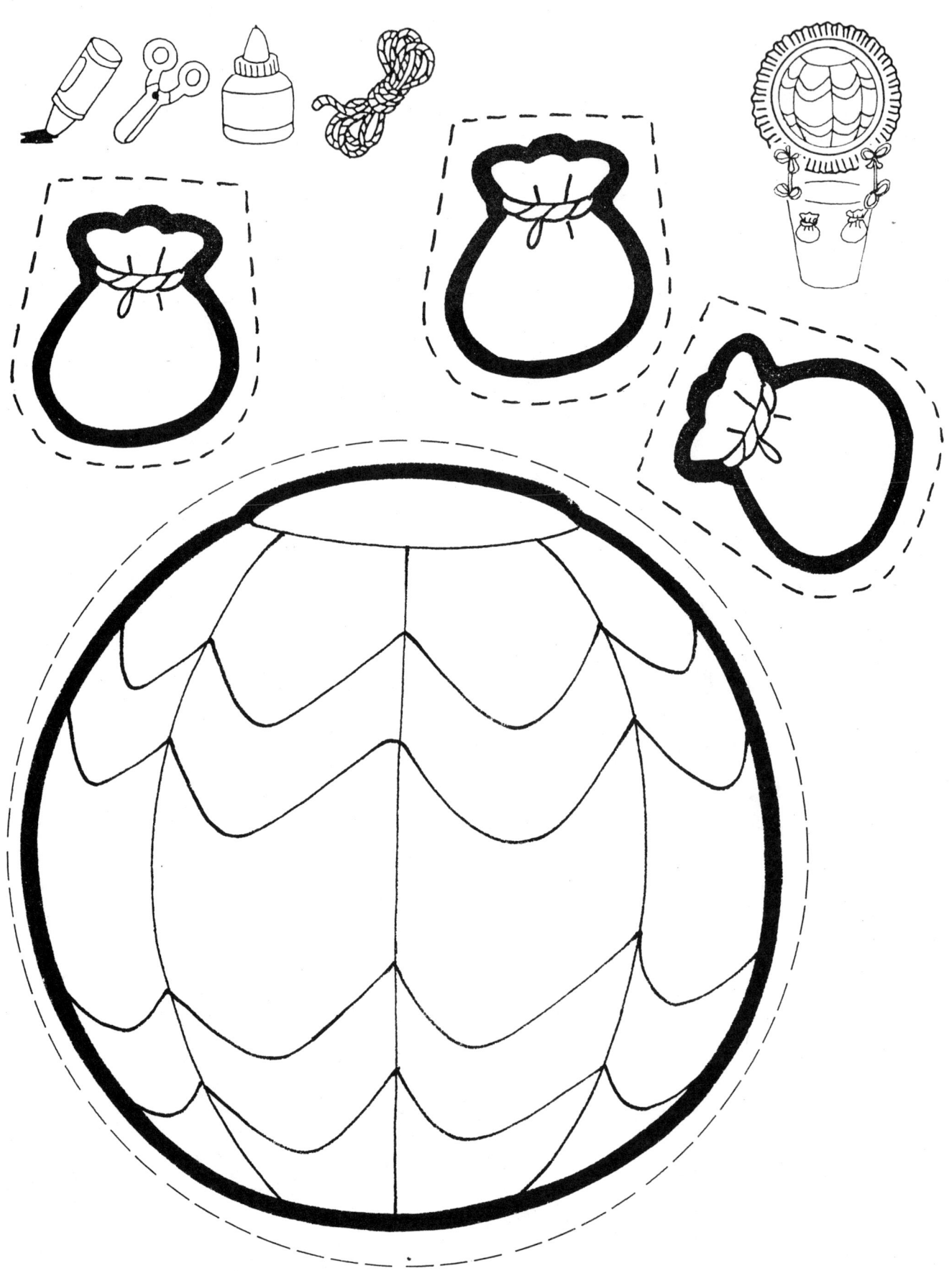